FASCINATING FELINES

Sixty Cat Poems

Hugh David Loxdale

BRAMBLEBY BOOKS

FASCINATING FELINES: *Sixty Cat Poems*
Copyright© Hugh David Loxdale 2002

ISBN 0-9543347-0-1

First Published 2002 by
BRAMBLEBY BOOKS,
Harpenden, Hertfordshire,
AL5 5HE, UK.

Illustrations:
Front cover: Watercolour by Kate Fasnacht
Back cover: Drawing by Ulrike Bauer

Printed in Germany for Brambleby Books by
*AZ Druck und Datentechnik GmbH, Postfach 3150,
87440 Kempten, Germany*

FASCINATING FELINES

Sixty Cat Poems

Poetry by the same Author:

The Eternal Quest (1988), Merlin Books Ltd.,
Braunton, Devon
(as Hugh Llewelyn)

Blue Skies in Tuscany (2000), Minerva Press Ltd.,
London

- *Preface* -

The first twenty poems were written between 1987-89, whilst I lived in Flitwick, Bedfordshire, the rest during 1995-2000 in Harpenden, Hertfordshire, with the exception of four poems (pp. 78 – 81), written on the island of Nevis, West Indies in October, 2000.

The following poems - '*The Cat*' (9), '*The Lynx*' (19) and '*The Huntress*' (36) - are reproduced from '*Blue Skies in Tuscany*', published in 2000 by Minerva Press Ltd. The poem '*Ghost of a Cat?*' (33) was first published in 1988 under the pseudonym Hugh Llewelyn in '*The Eternal Quest*', Merlin Books Ltd..

Hugh D. Loxdale

Harpenden, 6th July 2002

Dedicated to Joan Wheatley, a great admirer of felines

Contents

The Cat

A most excellent invention is a Cat,
With its handsome features, sleek coat
And hazel eyes,
And very good company too; most happy
For a chat …
With the added advantage (some would say)
Of being a good listener,
Giving few replies!

The Riddle of the Silken Cat

The silken Cat,
Appearing like the Sphinx -
Silent and inscrutable -
Sits, watches … and thinks …
But exactly what
Is hard to know.

It observes us
In every aspect
Throughout the day.

In moods of joy …
Or black despair …
In love, nakedness,
In tears, asleep,
Work, play, aggression, fear.

Perhaps the thoughts
That flow
Below its ruffled brow
Are magnanimous,
Reflecting affection …
Or maybe acceptance
At our behaviour …

It's impossible to say.

Or maybe even
Deep thoughts
About the meaning
Of it all …
And our role
As benefactors and guardians …
We large, imperfect creatures

Put on this earth (apparently)
To house, feed, entertain
And cosset
In every way
Throughout their lives,
Short relative to ours.

Or most probably
(Or so we would like to believe) ...
Their thoughts revolve
Around mere mice
Scurrying in the darkness ...
An abstraction
Made flesh by sound and smell.

It is an unsolved riddle
The ancient Egyptians knew well ...
Although similarly,
Could not solve ...
Such is the silken cat
With its strange, impelling powers
And which may hold secrets ...
But will never tell.

Cryptic, Crepuscular Cats

Cryptic, crepuscular cats
That crouch in the *Fuchsia* hedge …
Unseen as if not a leaf stirred …
As the Sun goes down …
Until one softly purred
When I approached …
Although made no other sound …
Waiting for encroaching darkness
To bring out
A Wood Mouse …
Or some similar prey.
A tasty morsel
To round off
The day.

Out of the Ether

Out of the ether
The harpsichord relays
Its ancient strains,
New presented.

The cat on the lap,
Washed in sunlit rays
Continues, at pains,
To look quite contented.

The man
With his book
Stares at the kitten
That plays on the floor,
As if demented.

A scene, fused in time,
Which could be now
Or two centuries removed …
Or a figment
Of the mind, -
Hence neither.

*Buster the Cat (*Circa *1941)*

Buster the cat of long ago,
Sits in the photograph
With a satisfied glow.

What joys he felt,
What mice he caught,
All is faded,
We no longer know.

Are they not Cats?

Hey chaps!
You are supposed
To be out
On the moors,
In the rain and fog,
Stalking mice - or whatever,
Not sitting here
In front of the fire
Attacking me
With your claws.

Are you not cats,
And shouldn't
You be seen
To be so …
Prowling, growling,
Fighting, howling?!

It really is not good enough.
But there you are,
They are my friends …
And it would be cruel
To turf them out
Into such a night
With mist,
As thick as a Fox's brush,
Swarming close by.

Even so, I get up
And open the several
Doors to let them out.
There is no rush.
Only the slinking purr
Of two contented felines

Stretched out,
Upside down,
Lit up by the crackling flames ...
And studiously ignoring
The recital
Of their several names.

*Very Good Wieniawski!**

Very good Wieniawski,
I enjoyed that …
And so did my Cat!

*On listening to Henryk Wieniawski's
Second Violin Concerto in D minor, Op. 22 (1862)

Upon lifting Wilhelmina

Upon lifting Wilhelmina
Whose paws were never cleaner,
There was a little purr
Deep below her fur ...
Like the last contented breath ...
Of an exhaled concertina.

The Lynx

Yes, indeed …
To some
The behaviour of the Lynx
Is disagreeable …
And stinks!

Cunning, predatory and cruel.

Yet then,
Is it not
The nature of the beast
To pursue, capture
And feast
On its hapless prey?

At least it is real,
Alive to the feel
And need of love and pain,
The Arctic wind and rain.

It is no mythical being
Standing on a marble plinth
To gaze down
Upon the world with disdain
And sterile aloofness.

I would say
It is true unto itself …
In courage and in stealth …
And he (or she) who thinks otherwise,
Is but a fool.

Turfing Out the Cats

It is a shame,
But there you go
Into the hail
And caustic snow.
You cannot stay
There all night,
Curled up asleep
In a ball, so tight …
Your pretty features
And fine coats
Will not save you,
You unfortunate creatures!

So out, out,
Away, be gone
And don't return
Until the morning Sun
Embraces the glorious colour
Of a hundred roses …
Which you sniff
Occasionally …
With sensitive noses …
But do not love …
As I do …
With a warm inner glow
Of pride.

Through the Eyes of a Stranger

Through the eyes of a stranger,
There is now little danger
As she walks up my chest
To stare at me closely
In the face, without anger.

Still, it is one
Full of ambiguity …
One I do not care
To dwell upon … too much.

Slit, amber eyes
That may water when
The cold wind blows …
But never fill with tears
From cries of lament.

Now her looks
Are fine and friendly.
Yet were I her prey,
What looks then
I wonder …

As she comes in
For the kill …
Or play a while,
And tear and rent
Asunder?

Such are the looks
Of a Cat …
One of a predatory race.

The Cat and the Butterfly

The summer air
Is still …
And very hot.
A white butterfly flaps
Lazily across the garden
From left to right.
Timmy, a big tabby
Is nearby,
In the golden shrubbery,
Concealed
Well out of sight.

Then in an instant
A ballet begins …

The butterfly swerves …
The cat leaps … (and grins) …
Up and down,
From side to side …

The butterfly, a female,
Avoids her pursuer,
Whilst Timmy,
Flicks his tail
And licks his lips …

A quick decision …
To swallow
Or chew her?! …

Though knocked to the ground
And held by a paw,
Her fate
Is not quite sealed ...

In a trice, she's aloft,
And gaining height ...

Only her legs
Are now fewer.

Here comes Timmy

Here comes Timmy,
A large and wicked Cat,
Who yesterday killed a Song Thrush,
For it, alas, that is that.

No longer to sing in the shrubbery,
Or call from a mighty Yew,
For now it resides in the belly
Of my friend, a tabby most true.

And although I have often scolded,
And reproved him from such cruel acts,
He laughs (from within) in his feline way:
'Oh these humans, with them what can we do?'

Semi-detached Cats

They are not worried
If one is cold, tired,
Hungry or old.

They are not
Amused by Voltaire,
Enchanted by Chaucer,
Transfixed by Mozart,
Or moved
By what
Scientists have foretold.

They are immune
From bills,
Taxes,
Traffic jams, shopping,
Washing clothes, -
And other such ills.

Nothing stirs their composition ...

With the exception of ...
A little love,
Hate, a stretch,
Yawn, walk,
Play on the carpet
By the fire ...
Or to be gently scratched ...

Or … the sound
Of imminent dinner
Being extracted
From its sealed tin …
To them,
A mouse in armour
Perhaps?

It seems they are
On to a winner
And choose to remain …
Largely detached.

Are you a Cat?

Are you a Cat …
And if you are,
Should this be so?

Should you not be
A lion or a princess?
I think you don't know!

True, you are
Dark and furry
With a swishing tail …
And look like a cat.

But I have my doubts …
And believe you are an illusion.
I think you're a vision …
A feline delusion.

Feeding Time

All right
You hungry, wungry Cat.
Hang on,
I'm coming!
Don't break down the window
Or door
With your unkind tapping paw …
Like Kathy
Back from the Moor!

Presumably you're starving then.
Don't rub my leg away.

Ah yes, meow, purr
And beg
Now …
But it wasn't always so …

As last night
When you growled
On being picked up …

And again, the other day.

You'll be fed, don't worry.
Don't be in such an urgent hurry …

Or I'll cut myself
On this infernal tin …
'Though I don't suppose
You've considered that …
You hungry, wungry cat.

Fascinating Felines

It is not true
That I particularly like cats.
Sure, I admire them for
Their agility,
As they admire us, no doubt,
For our clever ability ...
And for their exquisite beauty,
Their proud and haughty looks
As they us for our loftiness
And absorbing books ...
And for their cruelty
As they too, for ours
(Although I do not approve either).

Lastly, for their independence ...
For their sublime indifference
As to whether one
Likes them or not ...
Save at meal times ...
And when it is cold and wet
Outdoors,
And they seek
Warm places
To rest ...

Often a lap
At best ...
Before they drift off ...
To another land
Of great expectations:
Of nutritious mice
And other thrilling sights
And chases;
Benevolent, doting keepers;

Free love …
And freedom
To rest and play
Whenever they please …
Whereupon at length … they awaken
To find the world
Much as they left it …
A demi-paradise
Of earthly delights.

Samantha

A beautiful Cat, Samantha,
More mog ... than panther ...
Despite her black coat, looks
And cold golden eyes ...
Still, essentially she is a kitten
Much smitten with an old wine cork,
Or a hazel nut,
Which she bandies
For hours
With her large satin paws
Around the house.
However, soon now, she
Will attain maturity,
A security in knowing
That she too can fend for herself ...
And then wreak havoc
On the many poor unsuspecting
Creatures outdoors ...
The main preoccupation, it seems,
Of her terrible tribe.

The Cat That Never Looks Back

The Cat that never looks back,
As it departs fast into the black,
Its senses tuned to the night,
Its instinct … an inner insight.

And within that nocturnal world,
With claws duly unfurled,
It lays in an old apple bough,
Vigilant of all that's below.

And when, with the faintest rustle,
Are detected the movements of muscle,
It falls silent as a wraith
To pounce with all its faith …

On its victim, unseen in the grass …
A scuffle, a shriek and a gasp …
To be swallowed, swift as a snack …
Then it's back … to hunt … in the black.

Ghost of a Cat?

All I saw
Was a flash of ginger
Past the door.
On looking outside,
There was nothing there!
Not a sign of movement, hide
Nor hair!
It cannot be him, I thought,
Because surely he (the neighbour's cat)
Is dead.
Only last week he sat
In the garden, alas thin and lean,
A vision of pity
As I've ever seen.
Poor Tom, no longer
To sniff the lavender bush
In the wide flower bed
And purr …
And caress it with a warm, wide head.
I fear he was gravely ill …
Possibly, for life, he lacked the will …
So maybe somewhere lies hereabouts;
But by his owner
It's clear he was never loved …
For I notice
His loss is silent,
Met without cries or shouts.

Have you Fed the Cat Yet?

'Have you fed the Cat yet?'
'No, I only spoke of food, -
And then clutched her tightly
To test her hungry mood.

I mentioned birds ... and mice,
And acts of daring do,
But she was not amused
And refused to purr for you.

Her eyes gleamed a golden,
Her tail swished at length,
"Come on, do feed me (she said),
Or I'll quickly lose my strength"'.

Our Furious Cat

Our furious cat
Was out this morn
Murdering little birds
Amidst the roses
And other bushes,
And the listless herbs.

Thrushes, tits and Robins,
Naïve and newly fledged.
No pity or remorse
From her alas …
Can now at all be dredged.

On the door mat
She lonely sits,
Locked out and in a state: -
'*Persona non grata*';
Of her, we do berate.

The Huntress

A figment of the darkness,
This was her hunting ground …
The small garden
Where the hollyhocks grew straight and tall …
And lost their innocence … and hue …
To the blackness …
Where hardly a sliver of light
Now broke through
Beneath the still, rolling clouds
And the fickle stars
That refused to show …
To the bats
Whose shriek
Only she could hear -
Loud and clear -
The frogs that frequented
The pond
And splashed about, occasionally …
And on the lawn,
There she sat, paws withdrawn …
Waiting, waiting
For the first slight
Crack of dawn …
The first faint call
Of dove or swift …
Glaring amber eyes,
Staring into the hidden pitch
Where a mouse might twitch,
A moth beat its chocolate wings
In the heavy air, sticky as treacle

And warm … carrying
The scent of roses and lesser blooms.
There she sat, all knowing,
All seeing
In her little world,
Content as any being
Can be …
Where the blackness reigns …
Black cat invisible
To those foolish enough
Not to see
Her low, breathing form …
Or those washed embers glowing.

The Cat and the Bed

I caught her just briefly …
But then she quickly fled
Round the tall drawer
And onto the bed …

There to remain in perfect peace
On the loveliest blanket fleece …

Oh, though yet to spread her horrid fleas,
Despite my most earnest pleas …

Which brought about a soft reply …
'Do go away … and let me lie!'

The Finest Cat That I Ever Saw

She is the finest cat that I ever saw,
Mostly black … and two foot four
From the tip of her tail to her charcoal jaw
And black on her legs too, down to the paw …

These a snowy white as is her chest,
Very furry … quite the best
Pelt that ever covered an animal lest
It was adorning a lady on the catwalk pressed …

By money or desire to reveal her sleek form,
Whereas the cat patrols the Moon-green lawn,
Confident in her looks from dusk 'til dawn,
In the only fur coat that *she* has ever worn.

Action Cat

Ah, the Cat is showing activity,
It's sitting on the landing
Washing itself from top to toe
Awaiting its mistress with understanding.

At her strange behaviour in the tub,
Involving water, soap ... and singing,
Which it reflects is all very odd,
An evolutionary quirk, most intriguing.

Yet it's not philosophy that drives the cat
And its zealous toiletry striving,
More like breakfast from a tin,
Hopefully to be soon arriving.

And As For You

And as for you, you're just a Cat!
But a very fine one
All the same,
Whether on the old Indian rug
By the fire
That you have sat on
And clawed and snagged
Over many years …
Or seated comfortably on this chair
Where Nischi should rightfully sit,
Not now to knit,
But stare blankly
Into the coloured screen
Moving her mouse,
Of little interest to me
And too slow for thee,
As the soft evening hours
Slip quietly by …

Whilst you remain strangely serene.
Perhaps the hum
Of the computer
Makes you so?

In reality of course,
This sitting around
Does none of us any favours,
Least of all our once slender forms.
No doubt you think 'Oh why worry.
In these long days of ease,
Why can't we do as we please
And make this unlearned behaviour
One of the norms?'

Yes, so I can see …
And an over-stretched one,
As far as you are concerned!

Cat in the Birdhouse

In the birdhouse
six foot tall
Samantha sits
looking cool,
her tail hanging limply down
to twitch in the tranquil summer air.
How she got up there
is a mystery ...
until one day we saw
how it was done.
Literally, a bound at the pole,
then with claws out
she crawls swiftly upwards,
next arching around
to squeeze herself
into the tight space within.
We are 'tickled pink'
and tease her with a straw,
which she lashes at
with her deadly paw,
only, apparently,
wishing to be alone.
But I wonder
if the birds are so amused –
probably more confused
than anything –
and doubtless alarmed.
A fright for the Robins and tits,
Blackbirds and every finch
that must surely flinch
when they come in to feed,
suddenly to find
a large feline presence,
immeasurably frightening ...

So that they depart
like grease lightening,
which I can understand,
but which is doing our bird list
no good at all.

As the Sun moves
around the sky,
perhaps it is too hot
for her being so high
and mighty.

Eventually she drops to the ground,
effortlessly, without a sound,
to lie in the shrubbery,
still overcome, I suspect,
by the need to think
of more skulduggery,
now in a cooler clime.

The Cat and the Newspapers

Early on Sunday when the tea is made,
And the papers, unfurled, on the bed are laid,
Up jumps the Cat, more hairy than fat,
And on them proceeds to duly parade!

And just at the spot with the 'juiciest' bits,
There she stays and happily sits, -
Not that she's intending to read much right now,
Being more content to purr and meow.

But eventually when the time has come
For her to leave and seek more fun,
Off she goes, with a rustling sound,
As the crossword is trampled ...

And she's gone with a bound.

Cats May Sleep All Day

Cats may sleep all day,
Yet men must work ...
A cruel reality
That does still irk ...

Though when the Moon
Glows strong,
As the Sun grows weak,
Men mostly rest ...
And the Cats do speak ...

Meow and wail through
The dark, small hours
When the rain drives hard
And the wind long howls ...

Mice scurry
And the bats close weave,
Whilst the stars sparkle
And the shadows deceive ...

Above and amongst
The tombstones galore,
The Cats hunt with both
Tooth and claw ...

So that in the morning,
When faint rays arise,
On the patio
Is a lovely surprise:
A field mouse, its head
Quite bloody and chewed,
And a Cat there awaiting
Its Owner's new mood ...

At the sight of this gift,
For breakfast it would appear,
Not from a Greek,
But our Persian, I fear!

Contemplatory Cat

On the bonnet of the car,
a rover,
warm and recently exercised,
covered in mud and paw prints ...
and scratches too
(if only the owner knew ...
and perhaps she does),
sits the large ginger Tom ...
huddled, surveying from on high
all that is around
in the gravel courtyard ...
his kingdom ...
with its other cars,
red brick farm and outhouses;
fat chickens strutting
detachedly ...
and Aylesbury ducks from the pond,
for some reason,
attempting to swim
on the slimmest of streams
that trickles,
glistening and iridescent,
to the road beyond.
The first two Swallows of the year
flit and twitter above,
slicing the air like butter.
A Brimstone, gaudy yellow,
skirts fast the small orchard nearby,
bedecked with blossom,
in its sexual search ...
Whilst the wind,
more of a slight breeze, not quite mild,
when the Sun has gone,
ruffles the cat's thick hair

standing proud on its back,
its eyes watering just a little.
Later, the owner and her child
get in the car.
They slam the doors,
disturbing his contemplation;
turn on the engine with a roar,
so that he turns his head
to stare more in protest than anger
through the curving glass …
That he has to leave
his preferred perch, his throne,
taken from him, if only briefly,
without concern …
and a disrespectful lurch.

Doppelgänger Cat

Whose is this Cat that looks just like ours,
Who passes by in the sunless hours,
Who dares to stride across our grass,
Who evades the sentry (our cat) who lets it pass?

Perhaps she, our cat, is confused
By her likeness, as in a mirror, much amused?
Or perhaps it's a lover, a Tomcat that calls
To court his queen beneath our walls?

But alas he'll be disappointed, even dismayed
To learn that she was long ago spayed,
So she can't be a lover, nor he her child,
For he lacks that madness; his eyes are too mild.

Kaleidoscopic Cat
(*For Rebecca*)

During breakfast at Wheat Hall Farm
In came this Cat to ply her charm,
And up on the sofa in a flash,
There to parade her vivid splash; -
Ginger and black on snowy white,
No dread creature of the sunless night,
Not now, as she caressed her head
Against our fingers ... and then she said
A few words of feline greeting
At this opportune early meeting;
Purring loudly ... like a dove,
To soak up affection, or cupboard love?
Ears stretched sideways, whiskers bent
By these humans, Heaven sent ...
To admire and pamper this kaleidoscope,
So tormented, but we think she'll cope!

Owls and Pussycats

Our Cat sleeps on the carpeted floors,
Often near the busiest doors,
Where it loud and blissfully snores,
Its head resting on satin paws ...

There to black out of sight,
The faintest trickle of brightest light,
Until the time is well and right
For its sojourn into the sodium night.

Where every wide-eyed tiger prowls,
Along with hunting by the Owls,
Long-eared, the rarest here of such fowls,
Whose call reflects the last of vowels.

The Monster Cat

The Monster Cat, the Monster Cat,
Very furry and very fat!
And very impudent, some would claim
Sneaking to snooze beneath the counterpane,
Which she thinks we cannot perceive,
But the bump in the surface does her deceive,
So that, with a whisk, her den is revealed
And her 'Sentence of Exclusion', not then repealed!

Advice to a Cat
(on leaving it indoors)

You be good,
And you be true;
Don't make a mess,
Or you're for the Zoo!

'Old Fruit' Cat

'How are you old fruit?' he said,
rubbing her warm black fur brusquely
the wrong way
as she lay outstretched on the bed,
slightly soaked,
and staring blankly full ahead,
her yellow eyes a gleaming.
'What did you get up to last night?'
'Oh come on, do tell us.
Have you got a lover?
Don't be shy.'

But she was not saying,
only keeping 'mum' ...
and purring proudly
like a Geiger counter
that reacts with enthusiasm
to some source or other.

After a while, realising that
further communication was
of course futile,
and that she would not
give the game away, what ever it was,
he got up, closed his book,
and drifted into the bathroom ...
with a tuneful hum,
sung in a strange key ...
Bartók probably ...
Whilst she, suddenly aware
of her new found occupation,
her 'right' as she might have it,
curled up into a little ball
and began to snore ... loudly,

a prelude to dreaming ...

Her nightlife secure, and still cloaked
in mystery.

Mad Cat Day

It's all very sad,
But I have to say you see
That our beloved Cat
Has gone quite mad …
And is dashing up a tree!

Or rushing about the garden
With its tail firmly in the air,
Its black hair a bristling,
And with a demented sort of stare.

Which could be due to the wind,
Or the Spring now a rising,
Or the small green frog it ate for lunch,
Which I guess is hardly surprising.

Periodically it shows this behaviour,
I suspect it's a kind of sport,
Fun for it and amusing for us,
Certainly one we never taught.

Safari Cat

Galloping across the TV screen
With lions in close pursuit,
The wildebeest flee for their lives,
An incredible scene to shoot.

And our Cat too is in on the chase,
Her eyes glued to the spot,
Until a 'kill' is suddenly made,
Which makes her full and hot.

So that she rushes up to the screen,
Her out-stretched paw a ready,
To assist in the deadly game,
Her nerves steeled and steady.

Yet the hard glass bars her way,
There's a quandary what to do, -
As thousands thunder past her nose,
Each one a lunchtime gnu!

Prisoner Of Her Genes

Today she was a grumpy cat
More deadly than the male,
As I found out to my cost
When I tweaked her swishing tail.

And saw that gleam in her savage eyes,
That look of cool delight,
The stare of the ruthless hunter,
The stare that she was right!

And licking my wounded finger,
A scratch both bloody and long,
I reflected if I had teased her,
And if indeed that I was wrong.

Perhaps I had and perhaps I was,
Though I assumed we were old friends,
Yet wary is he that gets too close
To the heart that tears and rends.

Who kills for sport, as we so do,
And is like us in other ways,
Its instincts framed in ancient times
Well before these balmy days.

When on velvet sheets our pet does sprawl,
Her body lithe and lazy,
Resting now, but forever tense,
And even slightly crazy.

To wound the hand
That will feed her soon
And that happily strokes and preens,
But she, like us, is not so free,
Being a prisoner ... of her genes.

The Oxford College Cat

The large white cat
Crouched on its plinth
As I stared into its eyes ...
Not bloodshot red, nor purple-black ...
And thus it was a surprise ...

To see each one ... distinctly ...
Pale amber and azure,
Both translucent as a crystal,
All deep and clear and pure.

Yet it *was* alone and did respond
To my most respectful entreaties,
Whereupon it fell to earth,
Just as the last of deities ...

Meowing with a disturbing growl,
A mewing sort of cry,
So that I looked askance at this enchanted beast;
I swear it's not a lie ...

And before I had composed myself,
It vanished from the scene,
Maybe into the shrubbery.
Since then, it's not been seen ...

At least by me, although it is true
That I rarely visit now,
So maybe the cat does still exist
But in truth, I don't know how.

The Cat in the Long Damp Grass

Now there's a picture of innocence.
The cat lying in the long damp grass
By the fence,
Ears twitching in the evening breeze,
Its soft mouth chattering
Toward the trees …
And the birds
That sing sensibly
Out of range … and harm,
Whilst the Ring Dove
Repeats its message
In Morse,
'Dit da dit, da, da' …
A strange code,
Always the same,
Known only by its kith and kin …
And possibly the cat too …
Who hears them
In concert
Above the twittering
Linnet,
The hum of the jet,
Easy and bright orange
Overhead,
Above the screeching swifts even,
Oh so high!
And the motorcycle,
A noisy din thankfully
Soon to pass …
All the sounds and rhythms
Of this May Day
At the turn of the Millennium,
A hymn of nature,
And of course, soothing balm

To the cat ...
As it listens in the long
Damp grass.

Off to Work, School and Sleep

A ginger tom
crossed my path
this morning
whilst walking to work …
It darted into
the hedge
on the far side
of the road …
above the school
down the hill,
and the pupils,
now going somewhat
berserk as the exams,
just around the corner -
in June, I believe -
turn them to despair …

Whether to fail
miserably and to cry,
or succeed beyond
even their wildest
expectations …
To send them on their way
into the wider
scene beyond.

Meanwhile
the cat finds
its spot,
a little patch in the grass,
there to lie down
in bright sunshine
and bask …

To fall pleasantly
into the land of dreams,
after a cursory
clean and brush up,
a lick behind the ears ...

Without a seeming care
in the world ...

As the bumblebees
quietly forage
on the Cranesbills
nearby.

Barometric Cat?

We open the door …
and put out the Cat
into a night
predominantly black,
except for the stars
and a watery Moon,
not quite full,
as if it could shed
tears.
But it (the cat)
does not run off
into that patch
of darkness.
Nor does she
sit quietly
on the step …
to watch
in silence
as the nocturnal world
passes by …
the bats, moths,
beetles …
and youths
in battered cars,
and the police
occasionally in
pursuit …
in the little time
between ten and two
when the clouds
roll in,
heavy with rain …
to obscure …

As if she knew ...
and wanted to
turn back
before the door
shut tight ... and true
behind her ...

As if she could sense
what we could not,
nor the weathermen
tell; the brewing rain
showers to come.

As light came back
and the warmth
returned,
the ground
seemed dry enough.
Only the grass was
dewy wet
as the first bees
went about their
business of the day;
the doves cooed
and made love
on the eaves above;
the milk float
wound its slow way
down the hill ...
and our cat came in,
wet through and through.

So she was right
but never complained,
as she was duly fed

to re-charge her furnace ...
and re-set the barometer
in her head?

Cats Will Be Cats

Oh that's very nice.
Thanks a bunch!
When the Cat came in
Late this bright spring morning,
Gulped down her food
As if she had never
Been fed before,
And then rushed upstairs
And without regret … and little ceremony,
Spewed her lunch
On the bedroom floor!

I hate cats, I really do!

Then again,
It's what babies often do.
And they grow up
Into stars like you …
One to inspire!

So I live in hope
That the cat will reform …

And one day become as you;
A model of decorum …
And desire.

Bubbles

Bubbles was the Manor Cat,
Queen of all she surveyed
Who, when visitors came, was charm itself,
Oodles of which she displayed.

She would rub up against their legs
And readily share her fleas,
And purr and coo and roll around,
All to amuse and please.

She would gladly lead them to the drawing room
Where the ancestors adorned the walls,
And the formal gardens, meticulous,
The rose arches, statues and pools.

Yet she was the very devil cat,
Her heart as black as her pelt,
Who would suddenly strike and snarl
And hiss – a hatred is what she felt.

For which and why she was so cruel
No one could ever tell,
And it was not just her appearance
That tagged her 'The creature from Hell'.

We can only assume it was her background,
An incident in her past,
That gave this jade-eyed terror
A role … quite unsurpassed.

The Glorious Tinkerbell

Tinkerbell was nobody's fool,
As butch as butch can be,
Covered in scars from nose to tail,
A veteran of many a duel.

During winter time when the cold wind blew,
In front of the flickering flames,
He laid his head on the Spaniel's side,
The only true friend he knew.

But woe betide any other dog (or cat)
That happened on his patch,
For he was as fearless as a lion
With arched and bristling back.

And chase them then so he would
As fast as they could flee,
Down our street to its end,
And get them if he could.

With the Children it was a different matter
For they could prod and stroke him,
And lift him up and put him down;
He especially enjoyed the latter!

Only when his name was called
Did he shrink from public view;
He didn't like the choice one bit
And was not the least enthralled.

Eventually he was taken to the vet,
Too old to soldier on,
And given once that fatal jab,
Thus fell our glorious pet.

Upside Down Cat

Our Cat often lies upside down,
Her feet placed in the air,
With mischief written on her face
And a playful kind of stare.

But when you go to touch her
With a bare unwary hand,
She is still the huntress
As you will soon understand.

And cut you and scratch you,
An instinct wildly driven
That she inherited long ago,
With no quarter ever given.

Car Boot Cat

Curiosity nearly killed her
When you were filling up the boot
With all sorts of rubbish,
Despite her being so cute.

She could easily have remained hidden
In the boxes you were to dump,
And perhaps she would have gone to sleep
To be woken with a bump.

When the trash went into the skip
To be duly burned and crushed
At the county tip, a dangerous place,
When the load is calm and hushed.

She could easily have gone in with the rest
And been suffocated or torn to bits;
A sad end for our lovely pet,
The last of four such kits.

Luckily she is no fool
And before you closed the lid,
Wafted from the open back
And in the laurels hid.

Flying Cat

She jumped from the upstairs window
Sometime in early June,
It was very hot and she had had her kits
And was probably 'Over the Moon'.

Later, when I opened the door
She removed them one by one
From the old box in the hallway
To the *Fuchsia* and out of the Sun.

Whether she feared for their safety
Or the temperature was just too high,
There she reared her four offspring
Under a cloudless sky.

In a little den on the garden floor,
A return to the wild for all,
A surprising act, at least to me,
A response to its eternal call?

Amazingly they all grew up,
Happy, healthy and strong
And used to sit by the *Fuchsia* bush,
A love that remained quite long.

Only the youngest kitten did we keep,
The prettiest when full grown,
Black and white with a star-struck nose,
But so far it's never flown!

Fireworks

Who would want to have fireworks
on a night like this?
Why, it's morose!
And a gross
annoyance to our Cat
who would love to
go out into the night
I am sure,
but for the explosions
and the showers –
multicoloured –
that pour
from the drenched heavens.
There may also be fireworks
later on towards
midnight
when the show is over
and another starts …
between
the two rival Toms.
Truly then cruel sparks
will fly …
and fur too
no doubt,
if their ardent
howls are anything
to go by in the wee hours
below the Mulberry tree.
Only the scarred
faces and serrated ears
are testament
to their many battles.
The cost of territory …
and a queen or more;

maybe the piercing of an eye ...
Until next May ... or November
when the fireworks
again grace
the northern sky ...
We at least will remember,
and doubtless so will they ...
with the settling of another
old score.

Black Cat of the Nevisian Night

I have seen him twice now
As he slunk past in the night,
A metaphor of darkness,
His eyes the only light.

He glared at me cursorily,
A mixture of fear and fright,
As he merged with the shadows
And was lost from human sight.

Doubtless he is a local,
Who takes this path by right,
Though who owns this nocturnal phantom
Is as unknown as his stars are bright.

Freddie

Freddie is a tiny mite
Abandoned when rather young,
Who now sits on a windowsill
All mottled, save his tongue.

Whilst his eyes are clear and healing
After a cat fight quickly won,
But not by this scrap of sausage
Who has character and is lots of fun.

Though certainly not a bruiser,
Nor a showy type,
He did once see off three old dogs
And scared them one by one.

Lucky the Lizard eater

Piebald and friendly
'He would never hurt a fly',
But he would certainly kill lizards,
That we can testify!

We were sitting on the veranda
As the Sun quickly set,
And the lizards got bolder,
The clouds a disturbing jet.

Suddenly from out of the bushes,
As quick as a lightening strike,
The cat caught a green lizard,
Which it certainly seemed to like.

And carried it off in its cruel mouth,
Its tail hanging down,
To devour it at its leisure,
A creature yet half grown.

But then shortly afterwards,
As if nothing was untoward,
He, a tom called 'Lucky',
Resumed his usual accord.

And purred and showed affection
With yellow eyes ablaze,
A pretence of perfect innocence,
To befriend … and then amaze.

The Cat and the Hammock

The hammock looked inviting,
Slung by a placid sea,
The Sun in its final descent
To meet this tranquillity.

And as I prepared to climb inside,
To relax and watch the view,
The Cat beat me to it,
I'm not joking; it is true!

Lucky by name and nature,
Sprawled out to its full stretch,
I could only laugh at the impudence
Of this loveable, cheeky wretch.

The White Persian Queen

She crossed my path
All white with fur,
As thick as I have seen,
And gave me such a stern look
As if she were indeed a queen.

But to my surprise,
Then traversed the road,
And hid below a car,
To emerge a short while later,
Her ear tips as black as tar.

Hence she must have brushed
Some oily bits,
Most probably the sump;
Whereupon she quite disappeared;
She had given me the jump.

I have read much on evolution
And of jumping genes,
But this transmogrification
Was undeniably by other means!

Lion Tamer and Lions

The Lion Tamer,
Dressed in red and black,
Stands amongst his lions,
Which sit around him
In a semicircle
On their chairs,
His hand raised lightly,
Almost casually,
Grasping the lash.

Never his back does he
Turn towards them however, -
Even the old lion,
Whose eyes are not as bright
As once they were.

He cajoles them, stirs their emotions,
Comforts them, tells them jokes,
Occasionally cracks the whip,
Just in case,
On the sawdust strewn floor;
Makes them pay attention
To him.

They, in their turn, stare in incredulity;
Half in fear, half in amusement,
Maybe a little puzzlement.

One or two bare their pink and black
Gums, dribble saliva,
Almost break into a smile,
Yet reveal a long, ivory dagger
In truth.

All this week, the Lion Tamer
Has had a chill, a scarf
Wrapped round his neck
To stop him falling seriously ill.

His charges examine him closely …
For any sign of weakness,
Of failure;
Of horrible, incurable disease.

No one blinks an eye
As the lions do their tricks,
Remain largely silent, -
Except for a near imperceptible growl.

They bide their time …
And meanwhile continue to lick their lips
To a smooth polish.

The Cat Comes In And Out

The Cat comes in, the Cat goes out;
I get cross and start to shout, -
'Are you staying in or are you *actually* going out?!';
The Cat comes in … and then goes out.

Strawberry Days

My love sits at the breakfast table
Reading her newspaper through,
Eating strawberries one by one
As I frame a rhyme or two.

And suddenly she exclaims aloud
That she has found a house to buy,
But I am lost in my thoughts
And fail to then reply.

Drinking my coffee and looking ahead
I stare towards the calendar;
It still is June to my surprise
As I can see from the flowering lavender.

The morning passes, the clouds roll by
I stroll into the garden,
There to watch the swifts o'erhead,
A sight to always hearten.

And meet the Cat beside the hedge
Whilst I pluck goose grass just for fun,
Who stares at me in disbelief
As I work in the broiling Sun.

And finally it is too hot,
For she was surely right,
So I go indoors to rest awhile
With one strawberry left … to bite.

The Urban Panther

In the darkness of the jungle
Where the Black Panther strives,
All nature struggles ever forth
And only the fittest survives.

Similarly in the urban sprawl
With its roundabouts, highways and alleys,
A habitat that our cat knows well;
On this side of the hill she sallies ...

To sit and watch the world go by,
The children, cars and buses,
The smelly dustcarts and motorbikes,
Rarely, if ever, she fusses ...

Although sometimes takes terrible risks,
Rolling around in the road,
Certainly we often remind her
Not to become a squashed toad!

Yet she is now a veteran,
With eleven years 'at the front',
Her name, like her looks, Samantha,
Her nine lives preserved in the hunt ...

For mice and voles ... and spiders too,
Devoured with special relish,
I could go on and say much more,
But I fear I may then embellish ...

What after all is a remarkable tale,
Of courage and daring do,
Of luck and cool and lots more else,
And a tale so far quite true.